Fish Babies

Catherine Veitch

Raintree

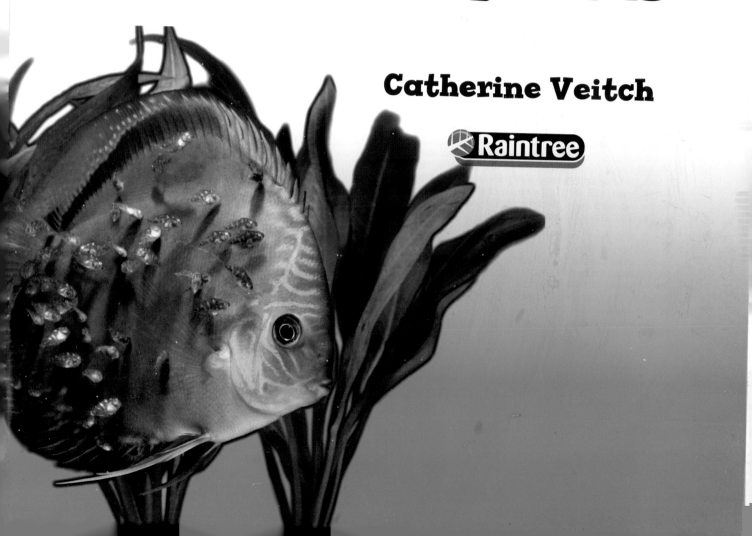

What is a fish?

Fish live in water.

gill

fin

Fish have gills. Fish have fins.

How are baby fish born?

egg

Most female fish lay eggs.

baby

egg

Sometimes fish babies hatch from eggs.

larva inside an egg

Sometimes larvae hatch from eggs.

Larvae grow into baby fish.

babies inside

Some female fish do not lay eggs.

baby

They give birth to baby fish.

Where do fish lay their eggs?

Female fish lay their eggs in the water.

Some fish carry their eggs in their mouths.

nest made from plants

Some fish make nests for their eggs.

bubbles

This nest is made of bubbles.

Caring for baby fish

babies

Some fish care for their babies.

baby

This fish carries its babies in
its mouth.

Some fish eat their own babies.

The baby fish hide to stay safe.

Growing up

Most baby fish look after themselves. They feed on insects and plants.

They hide from predators.

Life cycle of a fish

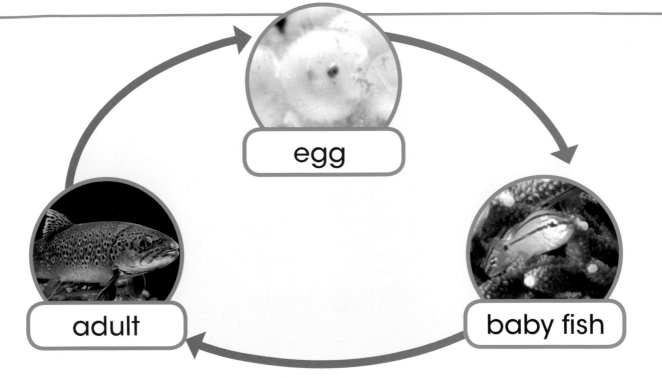

egg

adult

baby fish

A life cycle shows the different stages of an animal's life. This is
the life cycle of a fish.

Picture glossary

fin part of a fish that helps it to swim

gill part of a fish that helps it to breathe

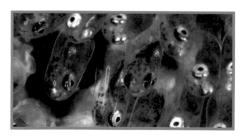

larva stage some fish have when they first hatch. More than one is larvae.

predator animal that eats other animals

Index

Notes for parents and teachers

Before reading

Show children a collection of photos and videos of fish. National Geographic and BBC Nature are useful websites. Explain what a fish is and discuss the characteristics of fish.

After reading

- Mount photos of adult and baby fish on card, and play games of snap and pairs where the children have to match a baby fish with its parent. Model the correct pairs first.
- Ask children to label the parts of a fish: for example, fin, gill, tail, scales.
- Look at page 22 and discuss the life cycle stages of a fish. Mount photos of the egg, baby and adult stages and ask children to put the photos in order. Encourage children to draw a life cycle of a human to compare. Compare how different fish care for their babies. Discuss the care human babies need.
- To extend children's knowledge, the fish are as follows: perch: p4; parrotfish: p5; bullhead eggs and fry: p6; ray next to an unhatched ray egg: p7; clownfish eggs with larvae inside: p8; pufferfish: p9; swordtail: p10, 11; cichlid: p12; jawfish: p13; stickleback: p14; Siamese fighting fish: p15; discus: p16; arowana: p17; platy: p18; trout: p19; grayling: p20; grunts: p21.